iii

"What we miss in today's world are thinkers," says author Amelie Diamant-Holmstrom. This trilogy inspires parenting, teaching and celebrating the uniqueness of every individual. Its pages are infused with values, the balance of priviledge with duty, of choice and freedom with accountabilities, of joy and sorrow, and calculated risk with experience and insight. It is a manual for the shelf of anyone seeking a richer, more meaningful life and who understands that the future of world peace begins as the generous interaction of each individual with himself and those around him.

Mark O. Hatfield
United States Senator - Oregon
Retired

In her new "Courtship of Life" series, Amelie Diamant-Holmstrom shares her profound ideas for revitalizing our faltering public school system. Her many years of teaching and thinking about the educational process has culminated in a thoughtful and provocative challenge to teachers, administrators and parents to re-shape the goals and purpose of public education. Amelie's fresh approach provides a welcome ray of hope that the joy of learning can be restored to the classroom. What a welcome message in these difficult times

Robert Bailey
General Director of the Portland Opera

Amelie Diamant-Holmstrom's "Courtship of Life" trilogy is unique. Her talent as a teacher, writer and philosopher places the reader, be it he or she, young or old, into a very personal interaction with the author, touching everyone's life experiences and suggesting new responses.

"Conversations With Thomas" is an empowering parent/child book.

"Destined For Greatness" is a wake-up call to rethink and reshape today's troubled education system.

"Yes I Can" is a book addressed to all who seek to lead a quality life - a book dedicated to putting civility back into civilization.

I would strongly recommend Ms. Diamant-Holmstrom's well-written trilogy to all who seek intelligence and education, while experiencing a near personal relationship with the author.

Fred M. Rosenbaum
Brigadier General
Retired

DR. EVELYN M. STRANGE

As a retired pediatric dentist, I have dealt with children for over fifty years. The "Courtship of Life" series by Amelie Diamant-Holmstrom, is a necessary instrument to revitalize our attitudes in communicating with children in a positive, joyful way.
Highly recommended reading.

Evelyn M. Strange, D.M.D.
Diplomat
American Board of Pediatric Dentistry
Associate Professor Emeritus
O.H.S.U. Scholl of Dentistry

EGO

ELLEN
GIENGER
ORIGINALS
ART-TO-WEAR

Straight talk from one of the most respected voices in education.
You will be inspired, empowered and helped reading "The
Courtship of Life" trilogy.

Ellen Gienger
EGO ORIGINALS

Contents

Dedication xi

Empowerment xv

Chapter 1: One does not teach a class; one teaches
individuals 1

Chapter 2: We are all each other's keepers 6

Chapter 3: With every privilege, comes a
corresponding duty.. 11

Chapter 4: It is the means, not the end, that counts in
the final analysis. 15

Chapter 5: Prejudice 18

Chapter 6: Creative teaching is opening doors 22

Chapter 7: It is both what you say, and every bit as
important, how you express your message,
that counts... 26

Chapter 8: To our students 29

Chapter 9: Growing from knowledge is more
important than accumulating it 32

Chapter 10: The personal touch in teaching 38

Chapter 11: We will be remembered not for what we
have acquired, but for what we have given. 46

Appendix: Positive school improvement suggestions......... 51

Message for teachers..66

Notes 68

Fund raising ideas you can use for your school...................70

Notes 72

My final thoughts and philosophy and teaching 74

Please respond with your comments:................................76

About the Author 81

Dedication

I dedicate this book to all my students, from whom I have learned so much and who have inspired me to write it; I dedicate it to *students* everywhere, who are an endangered species.

I dedicate it with love, respect and gratitude to my son, Eric James Holmstrom, who is the President of THING – O GAMES, offering challenging, award – winning, educational family entertainment featured at www.thing-o.com. It was Eric who first believed in my dream to *bring out the best in every student* and continuously encouraged me to write this book.

I dedicate this book to my son, Richard James Holmstrom, who inspired in me a sense of reality and purpose, a sense of generosity and adventure.

I dedicate this book to my parents. My father, Dr. Rudolf Diamant, a physician and dentist by profession, a poet and philosopher by avocation, who taught me to love, to dream, to hope, to try and try again against all odds. Most importantly, he taught me to live well, to laugh often, to treat myself well so that I, in turn, could treat others well. I consider my father my best friend, my mentor, the switch that lights my sense of values, of honor, duty, discipline, passion, compassion, of balance, and of *joie de vivre* – of joy.

My mother, Charlotte Diamant, an artist, a violinist and painter who inspired in me a sense of beauty, color and texture, and a curiosity about Nature's offerings – animals, flowers – and the magic they contribute to our lives every day.

I dedicate it to all parents – they who bring children into this world and only ask that the world will treat these human gifts with respect.

I dedicate it to administrators with the hope that they may re-shuffle their priorities from preoccupation with funding to promoting excellence in education by supporting and honoring teachers – *first* – for the sake of students everywhere.

Most importantly, I dedicate this work to teachers, our national treasures. Without empowered, committed, knowledgeable, dedicated teachers, our children cannot do their best. Teachers are the cornerstones, the mentors, the co-pilots of tomorrow's leaders – our young people.

Thank you "Lolamama" and "Rudipapa" for loving me.

To the far left, my mother,
CHARLOTTE M.DIAMANT
a talented violinist and fine arts painter from whom I
inherited the challenge to live life as an ongoing work of art

Dr. Rudolf Diamant "Rudipapa" my father, my mentor, my friend, my inspiration

My son Eric, continuing the "Rudipapa" tradition of excellence in education, playfully harassing me to finish this book

Empowerment

Come – create with me
Say what you have to say
Don't worry if the "form" is right
Just do your best today.
What matters is the content
What matters is the heart
What matters is the body and soul
that both produce your art.
We all have hopes and dreams—
even those who look for faults and seams.
Keep your head high and soar
Keep your heart warm with love
Walk through each open door
and like a gentle dove
Spread out your wings and fly
As high as the eye can see.
Oh, yes, you make a difference
as long as you are FREE!

Mme. Amélie Diamant-Holmstrom with her students

Chapter 1

One does not teach a class; one teaches individuals

After retiring from a full-time teaching career of more than thirty-five years, I have come to the conclusion that my passion for teaching and my very strong belief in *educating the individual* were and are the basis of a very rewarding teaching career. I credit my success to a childhood guided by loving parents and grandparents and caring friends.

I was born in Vienna, Austria and schooled in Vienna and Paris, prior to emigrating to the United States in 1941. Blessed with a rich intellectual background (my father worked and studied hard to become a physician specializing in dentistry; my mother devoted many years to become an artist – a violinist and a painter), I inherited the curiosity for and exposure to both science and art at a very young age.

I always considered my father, Dr. Rudolf Diamant (or Rudipapa, as we lovingly called him) to be my very best friend and role model. Although he was a dentist by profession, he had the soul of a poet and philosopher. As he and I were both early risers in my childhood, we spent many .a morning taking walks hand in hand, like Mary Engelbreit's Lion and Lamb – he, looking down with warmth, love, grace and wisdom and I happily trotting beside him, looking up in anticipation to listen and to learn from my loving, wise, gentle, tolerant, open-minded, visionary mentor.

In my native city of Vienna, we communicated and experienced life as a family. We (I am one of triplets) learned to listen and to share information at an early age. Our hearts were young; we were spirited, inspired and curious for knowledge and generously provided with knowledge and love. Our parents, family members, and friends were willing and able to answer our endless questions, and they always motivated and challenged us to try new things and to do our best.

I remember we always ate meals as a family; never hurried, we were encouraged to discuss our day, our triumphs and our failures. We were taught to *court life* by being made aware of our options, responsibilities, and consequences. We were taught to act responsibly and to choose as wisely as possible, to be grateful for what we had, and put our strength into improving it. "Court life and it will court you" – that was our aim.

I believe love, patience, knowledge, understanding, dedication, hope, commitment and humor are the key players on life's stage. They are the backbone of education and the essence of a quality life.

It was my father and mother who taught me that love – in its most complete sense, *caring* for one another and doing whatever possible to empower each other as total human beings – is the most important, the most rewarding and essential mission we can fulfill in making our life's journey a quality one.

The most important steps we are "privileged" to take are to profit from our parents' teaching and from our school education. To *listen* and to *learn* were always presented as gifts to explore, to act upon and to experience.

Already at a very young age (about nine) I always role-played as teacher with my triplet sisters and our friends. In Vienna we vacationed at a wonderful country place, terraced in three levels – one all in wild-flowers, and a second graveled with bordered flower beds and a grape-trellised gazebo. It was there that we played school, there that the roots of my desire to become a teacher took their first hold.

Taking daily walks with Rudipapa, my beloved dad, was like watering a flower-pot and awaiting its blossoms to sprout. Voltaire said, *"il faut cultiver notre jardin"* (we must tend our garden); this giant thought may well be the starting point and backbone of my teaching career.

Students are like seeds, entrusted to parents, teachers and counselors to water, to nourish, to guide, to shape, to daily shower with love and knowledge so that they may grow to become individually strong, beautiful, healthy blossoms who, in turn, can pass on their strength, their magic, their empowerment.

"Life is an inner song, realized and acted upon," said Rudipapa. In every person is that special magic inner voice that, if lovingly cultivated, will rise upward, express itself and become the melody that permits self-assured communication from the depth of the heart.

When I walked into my first French class after completing my BA and MA degrees in teaching, I knew I would have to take steps never written in textbooks or teachers' guides to bring out the best in my students. It didn't take long to realize that my major role was imparting to my students that I was there to teach each of them according to their own abilities and needs, and to inspire their curiosity for the subject at hand and for life in general (since no one subject stands alone, but all subjects are part of a life experience). I made absolutely clear that I wanted to move each of them from point A to point B – that is, to help them progress from their skill level at entry (whether advanced, satisfactory, or below-grade) to as high a level of achievement as they could accomplish within the limits of time and resources at my disposal.

"One does not teach a class; one teaches individuals," I said as I opened my first session, "and because of this belief in the individual, I invite each of you to be my co-pilot in our quest to learn."

On the first day of school, I would tell my students, "Allow me to help you learn, and teach me what you personally need, so that we both can do the best possible job." As part of my personal touch in teaching, I assured them that I needed to know as much as possible about their likes and dislikes, their background, hopes, dreams, successes and failures, so that I could rewrite the standard curriculum according to their needs.

Of course, this takes time! *Of course*, this is demanding! But it is also *so rewarding* – not in a monetary sense, since teachers in today's fast-paced American technological society are underpaid and undervalued – but in a deep-rooted, soul-satisfying feeling of making a difference.

Madame teaching her students JE FAIS UNE DIFFERENCE
(I make a difference) a song she wrote

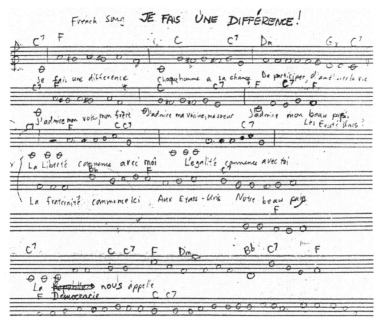

Chapter 2

We are all each other's keepers

Teaching is a work of HEART – helping young people to make intelligent choices. Education is not only about subject matter; it is about people being able to communicate, and to use the right knowledge at the right time for the right reason. You should choose teaching *only* if it is your passion; otherwise, you will not be successful – in fact, you could do real harm. In teaching, more than in any other walk of life, except parenting, love for what you do is the vital factor. We, as teachers, after all, are the catalysts of the individual's potential success (or failure); it is up to us as parents and as teachers to inspire our children, to present structure, commitment to excellence, discipline as a positive, empowering force, and to be their co-pilots as they chart their quality life journey.

An effective teacher does everything in his power to put a student at ease; he treats each student with respect and commands respect in return; he *listens* with an open mind and heart; he teaches with knowledge, love, and humor and makes himself available to the students, not as a buddy but as a friend.

Time after time, I realized I had opened Pandora's box, as the students unlocked and poured out their needs, insecurities, fears, hopes, dreams. (We are each other's keepers, after all is said and done.)

A case in point: A wonderful student of mine was truant four days out of every five; the administration and the teachers (including myself) were at the point of giving up, and the student was on his way to Juvenile Hall. I felt deeply that we (both teachers and student) were on the wrong path.

I invited the student to lunch, and as he poured out his pain I came to understand why he was truant, escaping to follow what he felt was his only path to happiness by hopping on his motorcycle and riding the open road where he could breathe and savor life.

I asked him what he treasured most and why, and learned that his passion was his motorcycle and his black leather jacket, and that his home-life was a disaster.

"Okay," I said, "I can hear your disenchantment and your pain. Please have your parents invite me to your home" [so that I could see and assess the situation for myself]. The invitation came and to my dismay I found myself tripping over beer bottles on the living room floor of this dysfunctional home, unable to communicate with the inebriated parents. My heart was in my shoes. I went home sadly, with the realization that the odds of bettering this boy's life were very much against him and me. Yet, for my part, I had to try, had to find a way to reach him and give him a chance to realize his potential.

The next time my student appeared in my class, I again invited him to lunch.

"I owe you an apology," I said, "I actually think you are a hero. I'm not sure I would come to class even one day in five, given your odds, but now that I've said that, let me negotiate. I will personally ride with you on your motorcycle, at high noon, wearing your leather jacket, waving to all your friends, if you will come to class four days out of five [which would at least be a substantial improvement over his previous attendance] and five out of five eventually. You have what it takes to become anything you choose, IF you equip yourself and take advantage of the education at your disposal. I am giving you an opportunity; please trust me, take me up on my offer. I believe in you!

"Now, order whatever you like for lunch, think about what I've said and let me know if you accept my challenge."

His impish smile changed to an open-hearted grin and he said, "You're on, ma'am!" What a relief!

"You made the right decision; why did you choose to take up my challenge?"

"Because, Madame, you're the first person who took the time to care enough to LISTEN to me." I quietly thanked God, and hoped and prayed for the best.

The moment of truth arrived; I cannot tell you how scared I was, sitting on that motorcycle! I held onto my student for dear life, as I smiled and waved, and prayed that I wouldn't fall off and be killed, but I had taken one of my calculated risks and it had paid off in every sense of the word.

I am happy to report that my young student did come to school four days out of five, graduated with a B-minus average, and went on to college and then to medical school. I learned this many years later when we met by chance at an airport; he introduced me to his wife and family, then hugged me and said, "If it weren't for this teacher, I probably would have ended up in Juvenile Hall or in jail."

There is no money that can pay for the satisfaction of knowing that you as a teacher have helped shape a student's future, empowered and inspired him to become a successful, positive, contributing member of society. This person made his way to the top of his potential in spite of obstacles, because someone believed in him.

We are all each other's keepers. Parents and teachers are in the privileged position to guide, motivate, assist and empower our young people to take charge of their destiny by using their inner strengths and their own special talents in making a difference. By the same token, we as mentors can learn from our young people.

Madame with her students discussing "With every privilege comes a corresponding duty." It is the teachers role to teach QUALITY LIVING as well as the subject matter

Chapter 3

With every privilege, comes a corresponding duty

I've always thought that to be an effective teacher, one must be constantly aware that one is a role model. This means acting, dressing, speaking with self-respect and dignity that inspire trust and respect from one's students, showing them the value of living with heart and intellect.

One must *live* one's beliefs, rather than preaching them; *lead by example*. This may mean opening your pocketbook as well as your heart. Small gestures – such as packing an extra lunch for a student who you know would otherwise go without, or giving up your lunch period to tutor a student who's fallen behind – these can make such a difference!

To share is to enrich ourselves: The more we give, the more we have. I made a little sign for my kitchen table: "Dear Guests: We'll gladly move over, set another place, and put more water in the soup, so please come back!" Happiness is having enough to share and bring the world together.

Empower the individual student to be an independently responsible and contributing member of society, able to share his strengths, hopes, and dreams, and to cope with life's challenges as he grows and widens his horizons in his quest for a quality life.

Learning is a *privilege*, the opportunity to fill your mind and soul with nourishing food that will strengthen you, empower you to live with *joie de vivre*, and enable you to taste life's fruits with all the juices intact. Learn early that learning is a privilege, a joy, an empowerment constantly opening doors and windows to fresh ideas.

We must *court* our students – that is, bring out the best in them and teach them to bring out the best in themselves, in each other and in us, their teachers, so that as a team we can achieve success for each team member and as a society. Knowledge is power – the educated players are the winners in life's game.

To do this successfully, we as teachers must begin with ourselves. We must equip ourselves with knowledge, love, passion, compassion, generosity and vision, to be worthy to teach. We must *like* ourselves and the teaching profession; we must fairly evaluate our own capacity to teach, and must be willing to open any door, seize any opportunity to bring out the best in each individual, emphasizing personal excellence and healthy competition.

* * *

"You have to pay to play," as Rudipapa often said. Nothing in life is free. For the privilege of learning, it is essential that students understand that their individual contribution – their best – is what is necessary to be successful. For every privilege, there is a corresponding duty. To do one's best and fulfill one's duty is, in turn, a privilege. Our best is the legacy we leave behind for our children. What satisfaction to be a teacher and a special part of the stairway to heaven; if the steps we build enable someone else to rise, we can take pride in knowing we have been a member of the partnership that provides a quality life.

We, who teach, must have the courage to take the calculated risk to find the best possible solution to each student's problem, to think creatively in our efforts to bring to our students as much knowledge, happiness, peace, security and beauty as we can.

In turn, students must accept their responsibilities to come to class with a receptive learning attitude, wearing appropriate and non-distracting clothing, and prepared with class materials such as books, pen and paper. Even the best teacher cannot create a fruitful learning environment when the students are disruptive, undisciplined, or inappropriately dressed.

*   *   *

Schools have a duty to encourage and facilitate parent involvement in the education of their children. Who knows the child better than the parents, and who has a greater duty to help them make the most of their educational opportunities? A brief, private parent/teacher conference, with a prepared question sheet to elicit specific, pertinent information about the student's interests and abilities for the course work, including any medical problems, should be a regular part of the school's outreach to parents. Whenever possible, *both* parents should be strongly urged to participate; an exchange of phone numbers between parents and teacher can keep communications open.

Madame lecturing in Paris

Chapter 4

It is the means, not the end,
that counts in the final analysis

After more than thirty-five years of teaching, I am convinced that the imposed concept of competition *at any cost* is more damaging than empowering. Experience has convinced me that the pushy anxiety that fuels much of today's ruthless competition is unhealthy. By the same token, winning fairly is sweet success indeed. When one strives for personal excellence at all times, competition can be a great learning experience.

Today's heroes and best-paid citizens are athletes: Run, pass, hit, get there any way you can, win at any cost – this is the message. Children are pressured to perform in so many ways, to "do" something, when what we miss in today's world are *thinkers*. It would be better to teach our children to think first, then to do, and to redefine competition as *competing with oneself*, and to simply enjoy improving upon our own personal best.

It is time to reconsider the ways in which we recognize and reward accomplishment: The truly great heroes are caring, knowledgeable, honorable individuals who base their lives on values and principles. Instead of overwhelming our young people with extracurricular activities which oftentimes merely replace responsible child care, let them contemplate the miracles of nature; let them open the window and invite thought to guide action. Action without thought is like gobbling food without digesting it. Action too often is reaction, which is fueled by fear and selfishness.

To win at any price simply cannot bring lasting satisfaction. Let us clothe action in thought, rekindle the light of moral courage, and teach our youth to think before they act. The result will be a world guided by carefully considered, reasoned choices, resulting in a richer future for individuals and for society.

We must teach our children that *it is the means, not the end* – the journey, not just the final destination – that counts in the final analysis: It is not enough to *do* something, to be first, to win at any cost. What matters is *how* we do what we do, what we contribute to the general good, what satisfaction we derive from simply being involved, as well as from the accomplishment of getting there first.

Rudipapa (my dear father, Rudolf) said that, to win unfairly while knowing your victory is at the expense of someone else's pain, is to lose. The materialistic world of today needs re-examination; parents must realize that giving time to their children is far more important than giving material things.

For example, the millionaire who buys his son a Mercedes, or the father who turns down a promotion because it will take him away from his family? What values do each of these children learn?

Today, we are unfortunately surrounded too often by man's inhumanity to man; we see anti-heroes glorified as heroes. It is time that courage, loyalty, a sense of fair play, constancy based on principle and conscience are re-introduced as measuring sticks for quality living.

We must act out of love, not fear; decency and integrity, not selfishness and greed. We must recognize and reward honorable accomplishment and hard work. We must be the courageous, dedicated, knowledgeable, loving, sensitive, caring, compassionate, honorable and empowering role models our children are seeking. To create our society's future heroes among our children, we must exemplify the qualities of heroes in our very own lives.

* * *

Students learning to share and to care about themselves, each other, their community and their world

Chapter 5

Prejudice

To combat racial prejudice, Rudipapa said that one need only realize that no child chooses his heritage. Knowing this, one can accept each person – white, black, rich, poor, Jew, gentile – on his own merit as a contributing individual, judging him on the quality of his contributions. Any one of us might have been the other person, but for the coincidence of birth; we are all children of God, entitled to the benefits this world has to offer, provided we pursue our opportunities and options.

To be prejudiced (the root word translates as 'pre-judge') is to be ignorant, uninformed and insensitive. To judge each person on his or her own merit is to be honorable and fair. Words such as *discrimination* have been misused; discrimination is defined as 'the ability to make a perceived judgment' – in other words, to make an informed choice. The negative meaning which relates to prejudice has for too long overshadowed the true meaning of the word.

Some people choose to improve their situation, while some choose to ignore opportunities for improvement; the latter are more comfortable in the role of victims, because improvement takes energy, hard work, commitment and responsibility.

Whenever you have a problem relating to someone's behavior, stop and put yourself in his shoes: Make the effort to see his accomplishments through his eyes, see his skills and shortcomings arising from his background. Then judge him as you would wish to be judged on the quality of his accomplishments according to having done his best, given his opportunities and how he has chosen to respond to these options.

I had a student who spoke unconventional English; he was from Africa. I soon realized that he was much in demand by the class; the students wanted to know more of life in Africa, to share this student's knowledge of survival, and to learn more about the importance of reverence for animals.

In turn, my students invited him to their homes, taught him about baseball and basketball, and invited him to movies and plays. This cultural 'cross-pollination' enabled him to respond to teaching and he was then better equipped to participate and interact with other students.

My students did not pre-judge this young man for his lack of "good" English; rather, they appreciated him for sharing his culture with them.

*   *   *

Respect all people: Rich or poor
Strong or weak
Straight or gay
Healthy or disabled
All races, all religions
People from all walks of life.

Learn to recognize, appreciate and fairly evaluate the contributions *each person* is capable of making. Realize that happiness and success require only that you do your own *best*. This is the art of living.

Language in action with my foreign language students
at the beach in Seaside, Oregon

Chapter 6

Creative teaching is opening doors

Students are the inspiration and the motivation for an effective, creative teacher. They are the *reason* for having chosen the teaching profession. We, as teachers, are privileged to be part of their growth process, and we owe them our commitment to excellence in teaching.

Excellence in teaching is giving our very best 1) knowledge of our subject; 2) personal attention; 3) role modeling in human relations; 4) respect and love; 5) energy; 6) humor; 7) willingness to listen to their input, their needs, hopes and dreams; 8) ability to communicate openly and fairly; 9) ability to open doors to learning; 10) guidance that will enrich, validate and empower them and those whose lives they touch.

As with any other vocation, to be successful you must know your subject well, love what you do, give your very best, and realize that each human being is special, with something special to offer you in return, that can expand your own horizons.

Teaching is elating, rewarding, depressing, even scary; yet if done with love, passion for learning, and compassion, the rewards far outweigh the disappointments. To be an effective teacher, one must dedicate oneself to the task with a feeling of love, hope and humor, feeling oneself enriched by the experience, not martyred.

The art of teaching lies in giving it one's all. To teach the students to look for the good, understand, reshape or eliminate the undesirable, to courageously take calculated risks and to learn and grow from each experience. An effective teacher brings out the best from each student, while equipping the child with knowledge and empowering him or her to use that knowledge appropriately.

As a Master Teacher for the University of California's Romance Language student teachers, I always suggested that the teachers put the class material in a colorful, appealing "gift wrap" – so inviting that students would be eager to unwrap it and taste the contents.

I always aimed to empower my student teachers to create a learning experience for themselves and for their students, by emphasizing the value of choosing from many sources of material and being ready to sift and mix their own knowledge with the formal prescribed course work. For example, I would tell the student teachers that to enhance the overall educational experience I would teach all the necessary foreign language vocabulary and grammar for a given topic in a colorfully cloaked fashion, and then form the class into small groups, with a gifted student as "President" and the rest of each group as "presidential advisors." Each group would then be empowered to take my material and enlarge and enrich it, presenting their version in a play, a musical, a reading, or a report.

I believe we must equip our students to be well informed, able to express their personal views in spoken and written words as well as deeds.

Creative teaching is opening doors. Give the students information, skills and techniques to furthur explore and appy their newfound treasures of wisdom.

Madame with her students listening to a speaker on
"How to Communicate"

Chapter 7

It is both what you say, and every bit as important, how you express your message, that counts

So said my Rudipapa, and his words still ring in my soul. So first think carefully what you wish to say, and then plan just as carefully how you are going to say it.

The skillful teacher makes the difficult seem easy, the tedious seem fun, achieving both with humor. The presentation of material is every bit as important as the material itself. From my own experience, I can tell you how much more one learns of a foreign language when, instead of memorizing the vocabulary terms for foods and tableware, one is asked to play at sitting down to dinner with friends, asking about the delicious recipes, admiring the artistic table-setting, making conversation on the social occasion.

Rote mastery of the assigned material is a safe but unconnected way of teaching; the aim is not to teach Language, but to teach Communication. Demanding perfection is counter-productive. It is far more visionary to encourage students to dare to jump in and say something, which can then be corrected if necessary, than to require them to only chime in when they have the 'right' answer.

An effective teacher reaches out to each student to elicit his or her best, and to let each feel enriched with contributing, while shaping each contribution toward the correct response.

The teacher who *empowers* the student to try and try again until success is achieved, who rewards each try while guiding the effort, is the one who will feel personally rewarded.

Teach with such conviction that you equip your students to be tough, confident, persistent, successful through knowledge, *and* flexible enough to accept new possibilities of their own.

A successful teacher is the mentor who enables the student to become the leader in his field. Government should be controlled by its citizens, rather than the reverse. Our youth need to be well schooled, well informed, able to act with knowledge, wisdom, purpose, courage, and conviction. We must offer our youth the tools to develop true standards of excellence for themselves, excellence which will inspire and illuminate those around them.

We all have invisible scars; some never heal. It is up to us as teachers to provide a psychological reserve bank account for each of our students – an account filled by teaching so effectively, so passionately, so personally, that the student stores loving lessons in his mind and heart to sustain him when things go wrong.

We must instruct, inspire, assist, motivate, and support them in their quest for and understanding of a quality life.

Madame at her home with her students discussing
"Bringing dreams to reality"

Chapter 8

To our students

To our students: Loving, caring, learning, daring, trusting, sharing, hoping – these are the gifts of a quality learning experience.

A quality life grows as we court it within us. We keep it in circulation by sharing it. We all have dreams; the conscious effort to bring these dreams to reality can cost a great deal – time, hard work, commitment, responsibility, and sometimes money – but *not* making the effort costs more.

To achieve a quality life, one must be willing to dare – to take calculated risks. The quest for a quality life is within your grasp.

Every action has at least two sides; it takes courage to view our actions from various sides, to keep what is profitable and discard what is counter-productive, realizing that nothing is all good or all bad. Personal happiness lies in discovering the balance point, the reality of joy that balances the pain.

The learning process and its gift, growth, make life's journey meaningful. Don't just work *hard* for a living: Study! Learn! Work *smart* – think before you act. Examine your opportunities, possibilities and resources for a meaningful, satisfying lifestyle.

My message to each of my students through the years has been, "Never underestimate your own contribution; no matter how small it may seem to you, it just might be the one item that makes the big difference in the total picture."

Take clothes design as an example: One might think the basic design, the suit or dress, is the main event, but often it is the special buttons, the unusual belt, a border, a cuff, or a special accessory that can prove the difference between ordinary and exceptional.

I try to point out to my students that it matters less whether they succeed every time, than that they participate in the fulfillment of their project, or dream, or wish. Knowledge is a gift that one must recognize, pursue, and apply, always leaving the door open for further improvement.

Madame with her students introducing multiple resources

Chapter 9

Growing from knowledge is more important than accumulating it

It is time for each teacher to ask himself exactly what he wants learning to be, and to fashion an exciting method to put this Learning to work. Teaching is a bit like acting: No matter how complex the subject matter may be, there is always a *creative* way to present it, costuming it to please and intrigue the student, motivating him as he listens and responds.

A successful teaching experience requires you to:

- ❑ set goals, construct a lesson plan, tailored to your class
- ❑ provide *personal help* as your students ask questions or need help in problem solving
- ❑ inspire *discipline*
- ❑ motivate *creativity*
- ❑ *praise* work well done
- ❑ create *fun thinking activities* such as plays and story-telling
- ❑ invite guest speakers, to *stimulate* varied approaches to learning
- ❑ *guide* students toward the ability to determine for themselves what is essential

❑ introduce *multiple resources* to give meaning to the material (i.e., films, tapes, library and Internet research to expand in-depth knowledge, bringing in outside experts to explain real-life applications of the subject of study, etc.)

Each student holds in his heart a space that he wants to fill; a challenging teacher provides the content of that space.

The skilled teacher recognizes the student whose inner space is waiting to be filled with the right knowledge and material, as well as the student whose space overflows with immaterial information in need of updating or enhancing. This skilled teacher courts each student with the knowledge appropriate to his needs, saying in effect "I am the person with my own *special contribution* that helps you, with *your* special contribution, to participate in an enriched 'we' experience."

One of the key lessons for a student to absorb is the art of careful listening; to listen to someone and to hold your ground with a mind open to other possibilities. This is one of the most difficult yet vital skills to master and put into practice. Having mastered this skill, however, one is on the road to success. This is why it is so important to empower each student to choose as wisely as possible the knowledge to fill that empty space – not to blindly take on the teacher's thoughts, losing his own on the way, nor holding the teacher's input at arm's length to protect his egocentric world and so stifling growth. This reciprocal communication of ideas after careful and attentive listening builds critical thinking and analysis skills.

Madame with her students watching a film on self respect,
self confidence and persistence

It takes values such as self-respect, self-confidence and persistence on the part of *both* the teacher and the student to empower the students to weave their own tapestry of the subject material. One of the most rewarding contributions a teacher can make to a student's success is to allow him to realize that growing from knowledge is more important than accumulating it.

Yet one can't ignore the importance of educational outcome as it relates to standardized progression within a school system to legitimately advance from grade to grade.

This should not be confused with rewarding a student on the basis of mere 'self-esteem' – which has become a politically correct code phrase for lowered expectations of hard work, commitment and scholastic responsibility. These expectations originally existed to advance a child as he reached a certain standard within a grade and was prepared to proceed to the next grade, to continue his growth within the subject matter.

In the name of self-esteem, some teachers and school systems today pass students to the next grade despite the fact that they are ill equipped in the subject matter; the fallacy of this well-intentioned but wrong-headed political correctness and catering to what some parents and teachers believe is the child's self esteem, reveals itself in the student's inability to participate at the new grade level. This, in fact, seriously undermines a child's realistic assessment of himself, since the real world beyond school is neither gentle nor kind to those who are ill prepared.

Getting money for moving bodies through the system, instead of actually educating students, perpetuates a false set of incentives and undermines the school system.

Success is only success if based on realistic grading, founded, in turn, on solid accomplishments and demonstrated mastery of subject matter. All too often, students are receiving grades they haven't earned – as reflected in the number of high school graduates who cannot read.

*   *   *

A sense of humor is as valuable as a pot of gold – more so, since gold may be lost or squandered, while humor constantly empowers you and enriches your life and the lives of those you touch.

A sense of perspective – that ability to take yourself and others seriously but not too much so – is essential to excel at teaching *and* learning. My beloved Rudipapa always said "Anything that is excessive – even if it is good when in moderation – can be unproductive, because it unbalances the equilibrium."

A student who studies all the time, gets straight A's but doesn't take time to relax, to play, to listen to music, to draw, to play sports – to enjoy life – will not be a satisfied, happy individual. We can help our young people set realistic limits to enhance the quality of their choices – and thus increase their enjoyment of each day as a gift.

I had a student who excelled on language tests, yet he never seemed to laugh from the heart or cry from the soul. He was enrolled in every possible course, and mastered them all, yet his eyes never showed a glow of contentment. I invited him and his parents to my beach house one weekend; they were delighted that I took such an interest in their son's education.

We all walked on the beach, sat and threw stones into the pools and watched the rippling circles. We ate, sang heartfelt songs. I saw a bright, genuine smile on the student's face such as I'd never seen before. The wind caressed his being, the moon rocked his playfulness into action, and the stars lit a bright new path for him. My too-serious pupil became a "Mensch" that weekend – a person whose feelings were unleashed, an individual who had discovered that to be unscheduled and free to receive life is far more enriching than to be over-scheduled, running to keep up. My student's parents were happy to share their son's educational experience.

One must take the time to digest life's offerings, rather than gobbling them frantically for fear of missing something. Our weekend was an eye-opening experience for my young friend, who later in life became a caring, brilliant, compassionate, nature-loving veterinarian.

Chapter 10

The personal touch in teaching

Overexposure to information can be as destructive as isolation and ignorance. In this over-informative machine age, the personal touch too often gets lost. We hear too much, not too little. We are bombarded by scenes of violence and crime – in print and on television, as news or "entertainment" – until we can become desensitized to suffering.

Let me suggest "rationing" television viewing time, and exploring instead the *quality* of the special people in our lives, while limiting and filtering the quantity of the outside influences on our lives and those of our children. This helps nurture a healthy self-respect; treating ourselves with kindness gives us a solid center from which we can reach out to others.

The personal touch in teaching is only feasible if we are happy with ourselves and genuinely like ourselves. The personal touch must affirm the importance of good physical, mental and spiritual health. Each year, each of my classes writes an original play, in which they illustrate the basic principles for this healthy life; I give them vocabulary and grammar to establish the basics of diet, exercise and spiritual inquiry.

I encourage my students to take a day of rest and recuperation at the first sign of actual illness, rather than ignoring symptoms until the condition worsens and forces a week's missed class time. Mental health is nurtured by honesty, integrity, laughter and tears to unleash inner enthusiasms and anxieties. Spiritual well-being is encouraged by quiet walks, relaxation exercises or yoga, swimming or any sport of their choice, and talks with God (God as the Higher Being, the source of support and empowerment greater than ourselves).

An effective mentor personalizes the curriculum to the individual needs of his students. In my own classes, this begins with my asking each person to write an 'autobiography' stating who they are, where they fit in their family, what they love to do (as well as what they *don't* like to do), family traits they enjoy or dislike or fear, what they expect from me and from the class, and how they can make their special contributions to enrich the class experience (and mine as a motivating and inspiring teacher).

I study these biographies carefully, and customize as much as possible the curriculum to be covered, according to the needs of each class. Although this is time-consuming initially, in the long term it is a most rewarding, helpful, and time-*saving* teaching tool. It eliminates losing students due to lack of interest in a 'one-size-fits-all' lesson plan for all classes, and assures participation because each student is invited to contribute his or her best according to their needs for the program.

In more than thirty-five years of teaching, I have lost only three students using this method. They were physically or mentally incapable of following the personalized language learning program.

*   *   *

The most empowering words one can utter to a student are

YES, YOU CAN!

To help a student progress, praise what he has done well, and offer reachable new options and challenges.

Success breeds success; praising a student for contributing motivates him to earn that praise again. An essential ingredient in motivating students is an atmosphere of mutual respect and enjoyment of learning. Eliminate the fear of trying by allowing initial mistakes (which, when gently corrected, are the springboards to progress); this fosters the teacher's role as mentor, and creates the climate for students to grow.

Let each student know that the ultimate proof of success is to be at peace with himself by doing his best which includes being flexible, willing to explore new options and to adapt to new challenges. Success is not a destination. Success is an ongoing journey. Help each student to look within himself honestly for that personal best. Tell him "I will be standing by – I will be here for you – you *can* make it happen – I will help you help yourself."

*   *   *

Teach each student that looks can be deceiving, although they can be appealing and serve to connect us with each other initially; that the best measure of potential and of lasting achievement is substance and contribution, not merely appearance; that actions speak louder than words; that differences of input make us each unique and, if positive, can contribute to our progress and happiness.

Life offers us opportunities, moment to moment, to release our hopes, dreams, fears; not to release them is to remain imprisoned by them. Allow your students to release their troubling feelings as well as their joys, thus facilitating their search for their best selves.

Teach your students to rejoice in their own successes *and* those of others; let them know that jealousy reduces the individual to his most childish and possessive self, while generosity ennobles and empowers. The more accepting one becomes of oneself, the more generous one can be to others.

Teach that the key to personal transformation is simply to be open to change.

All growth is based on the balance between rest and activity; let your student know it is as important to take time out to think, to dream, to enjoy, as it is to be actively involved in something.

Let your students know you don't expect them to be invincible; allow them to be vulnerable and aware that we all are independently responsible, yet we need each other's love, help, trust, and support.

Empower your students with understanding to let go of self-destructive habits. By helping them focus on their skills and strengths, you will ease their fear of the unknown, releasing old self-destructive behaviors, and you will empower them to trust themselves to improve. Encourage the repetitive reinforcement of character-building habits, formed by desire and education.

Unconstructive criticism is threatening and actually diminishes performance; positive criticism is empowering and opens doors to progress. To get at the truth, don't put the student on the defensive.

One of the major roles of an effective teacher is to be a sounding board, and then a guide to enable students to make meaningful choices and reach satisfying solutions.

Case in point: I had a student who needed French because he was invited to spend a summer vacation with a French family whose son had visited America on his summer vacation. I asked my pupil what his friend's family did for a living, who their social contacts were, and what he wanted to share with them in particular, to contribute to their growth, joy, and welfare. I learned that the parents were artists; they lived in Paris, and their social contacts were with other artists as well as with professionals and non-professionals of all walks of life. They were an intelligent, open-minded, creative family.

I went to the library and equipped my student with basic knowledge of the lives and major contributions of artists, and a simple vocabulary to meet the need to converse with his host family. I suggested my pupil choose five artists, and be able to talk about their lives and their paintings in simple terms; I encouraged him to ask questions if he didn't understand something, and told him not to be afraid to contribute, since that is the best way to learn. I also included a general vocabulary for everyday living.

Having tailored a 'survival curriculum' to these needs I sent my young student on his way, asking him to jot down in simple terms what he had learned, by keeping a diary, short and informative.

Upon his return from France, I learned that my student's limited knowledge of discussing the arts had actually endeared him to his hosts, and after reading the diary of his daily activities and comments which he shared with me, I was again convinced that a little preparation and a lot of good will go a long way to better understanding among people.

If you as a teacher can encourage students to see and be ready to accept what comes and make it work, you are a treasure. To empower students to be receptive moment to moment to the offerings of life is the mark of a dedicated teacher; to help them deal positively with the situation at hand is the mark of a caring friend.

*   *   *

Pause with cause; take control of your life. Teach students that each person has a limited amount of energy, and that the art of living is to use that energy toward what they can change, rather than wasting it on what cannot be changed.

Teach the empowerment of knowledge, by pointing out that growth is directly linked to learning and thus to knowledge. Acting according to knowledge is a source of power that leads to excellence.

An effective teacher is an important source of a student's growth and development; he or she guides generously, without prejudice, enabling the student to embrace life with an open yet critical mind and an open heart. Acting on these principles, the student has the satisfaction to become a creator and an architect of constructive action. With gentle intervention, a teacher can overcome rigid resistance, build trust and self-reliance, and enable the student to exercise leadership.

A true educator empowers students to make things happen, rather than making things happen himself; he helps students to help themselves. His enthusiasm encourages his students; he knows that outshining his students merely inhibits them. Acting as a director, he enables the students to be the 'stars.' It requires knowledge, commitment, dedication and integrity to lead students to become leaders in turn; an effective educator knows that real leadership consists of doing less by edict and doing more by example, and of letting the student be more.

A dedicated, self-confident, knowledgeable teacher leads students to learning as if to clear, flowing water, and enables them to drink. This type of teacher knows he is very, very rich indeed; he bathes in the glow of the many candles he lights.

The key to accomplishment is to take the first step, to get started, and keep moving forward. Empowering students to get started is empowering growth – growth that spreads from a central point of action in a ripple effect.

Teach your students: Life is an adventure: "Go out and embrace everything that is amazing. Take life to a new level: Be all that you can be with your own potential."

The personal touch in teaching

Teach with Knowledge and Passion
Live well
Laugh often
Love much
You must LOVE to be there
You must RESOLVE to be there
I was there, I LOVED it
I still love it – To teach is a joy and a privilege!

Chapter 11

We will be remembered not for what we have acquired, but for what we have given.

Let me close with a few words for our school administrators: Our schools would be far more inviting, our courses far more effective, if you would consider my method of *listening* and honoring the input from your teachers. Power, according to the personal touch in teaching, should be used as wisely and as sparingly as possible.

It takes a loving heart, an open mind, and the courage to *listen* and *make changes* when necessary, to make a successful learning experience for our students.

In a school hallway recently, I observed a principal so taken with his own importance that he attempted to solve a problem without taking time to listen to either of the parties involved. A teacher had stopped a student who was in the hall (against regulations) during class period; the student was attempting to explain the reason why he was late to class and in the hallway: He had just taken his mother to the hospital. The principal arrived on the scene, and in a very presumptuous, insensitive and self-important manner barked, "Don't stand in the hall – just go to class." The student and the teacher were both embarrassed and made to feel devalued and diminished.

Teachers are your best information sources and allies, if you will listen to them and treat them with respect. None of us is God; each of us is on an ongoing journey of personal growth. To be successful, we must put our egos aside and derive our reward from empowering each other in the quest for the best in education.

Great teachers are the backbone of our nation; teaching is the noblest, the most time-consuming, and most difficult profession. It is also the most important profession, if we are to have healthy citizens to sustain our neighborhoods, our communities, our nation, and our world.

Please work for a first-class teacher recognition/teacher education/teacher compensation system, to which the whole world can turn with admiration. We have plenty of resources; we simply must re-shuffle our priorities. People are willing to pay more for an excellent product; this holds true for education, as well.

At the end of our journey we will be remembered not for what we have acquired but for what we have given. Life's greatest gift is love. What lives on is the love we leave behind through our example of living what we teach.

*   *   *

Words and Music By Amelie Diamant Holmstrom

Love Lights The City

Medium Swing

City, Love with a song! All rac - es and re -

lig - ions blend and do be - long.

BRIDGE: Of course, we have our problems
                   We need to learn and grow
                   But what, indeed, are problems
                   As long as we all know...that...(Here in Portland, Oregon)

VERSE: Love lights the city,
                   Love leads the way,
                   Young, old, rich or poor,
                   We're here to stay

BRIDGE: We're elephants, we're donkeys
                   We're lions or we're lambs
                   We're tough or we are gentle
                   But all of us are champs...cause...

VERSE: Love lights our city,
                   Love leads the way,
                   Tall, short, fat, or thin,
                   We're here to stay.

BRIDGE: The dedicated people
                   All women and all men,
                   The healthy, the disabled
                   They all know that they can...through...

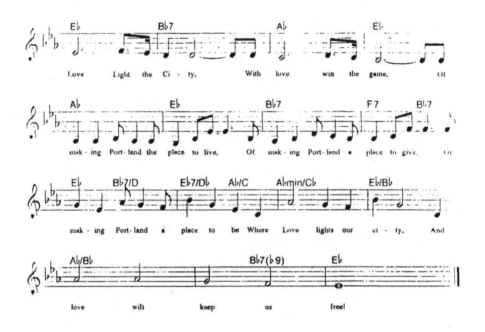

Love Light the Ci - ty, With love win the game, Of

mak - ing Port- land the place to live, Of mak - ing Port- land a place to give. Of

mak - ing Port- land a place to be Where Love lights our ci - ty, And

love will keep us free!

Love Lights The City--Words and Music by Amelie Diamant Holmstrom--Copyright 1993--Page 3

50

Appendix
Positive school improvement suggestions

I am still actively involved in education. These are my opinions about our nation, regarding education, based on my own observations and experiences. I believe these personal experiences have relevance to values affecting the future of our children. We are living in a democracy which offers us the opportunity to develop a wide range of skills, interests, abilities, responsibilities, values, and paths that lead to definite goals. We have hopes and dreams that we want to materialize.

I am, by predisposition and interest, more of an artist than a scientist, but I always understood that what works for me may fail for someone else. Offering knowledge, leaving it open to my students' various input resulted in a growth-enriching teaching experience for me, as well as a stimulating learning experience for each special individual student.

1. Rethink and redistribute available funds, moving them away from building funds and toward learning tools.

The important thing is to include a clause that enables funds to be "prioritized" in response to immediate needs – books, tapes, school materials, bonus awards for effective teachers, workshops that specifically deal with teacher empowerment and student empowerment.

2. Ban food and beverages from classrooms - lock the food machines during class periods (eating in class is rude, disruptive and counterproductive).

Ban junk food machines from schools. The junk foods are extremely unhealthy, contribute to obesity epidemic and cause sluggish thinking. Surely revenue can be found elsewhere! Some public schools allow food and soft drinks in their classrooms– "at the discretion of the teacher," according to several of the Principals I spoke with - what a cop-out! The foods are junk - chips and candy and sodas from vending machines that bring money into the schools.

How can one teach (or learn) effectively when some students are distracting the class by eating and drinking, or spilling soda on their books?

One of the principals told me, "It takes time to make changes...there are so many priorities." It would actually take only one directive to make a change! This cop-out by the principal puts the teacher in the individually awkward position of having to choose to be "cool" or "uncool" to the students, and the students are not seeing consistency. The principal sets up the teacher for failure, whichever choice is made, in this no-win situation.

When I walk into such a classroom as a substitute teacher, I say "Let me invite you to put away your food and your drinks so that I can teach you and you can concentrate and learn." I have never had an objection stronger than "but our teacher lets us eat and drink in class..." My reply: "Today, I am your teacher. Please trust me: it is in your best interest not to eat or drink during class - that way you can give your full attention to the material at hand. I love to teach and I want you to learn – that's what the taxpayers are giving their hard-earned money for."

I have not had any resistance after my little speech; it's not what you say, it's how you say it. We surely can find ways to pay for education that do not depend on installing unhealthy junk-food machines! This type of situation *can* be resolved quickly; as usual, it takes thought, commitment and guts.

3. Give special awards and recognition to
    a) outstanding teachers
    b) outstanding students
    c) outstanding staff

4. Get Parents Involved!

As a teacher who has keenly observed children and their families for more than three decades, I suggest that schools *court, invite and involve parents* in the education process as early as possible.

Schedule an Open House within the first two weeks of the school term. Mail an announcement to each home, including a form to be filled out and brought to the Open House, which will be the basis for establishing an on-going dialogue between parents and teachers about the child's

❑ health
❑ special skills and abilities, as well as shortcomings

❑ place in the family – siblings? other children in the home?
❑ social behavior, attitude, disposition
❑ goals, hopes, dreams – and commitment to these goals
❑ ability to respond to constructive criticism, response to loving discipline
❑ hobbies and free-time activities
❑ scheduled activities outside school
❑ likes and dislikes
❑ triumphs and failures (and ability to turn failures into triumphs)
❑ capacity to learn facts, digest them, and think creatively
❑ home activities in the family (meals together, family projects, games, etc)
❑ dress code
❑ self esteem, self image (introvert? extrovert?)
❑ travel experience, exposure to art, to languages, etc.
❑ parents' occupations
❑ extended family (grandparents, aunts, uncles, cousins) as 'support network'
❑ access to *quality time* with parents and/or extended family

This thorough exploration of each family situation helps demonstrate the school's and the teacher's commitment to each child as an individual. It forms the 'data base' for the partnership between school and family to provide each child the life skills necessary to a quality life.

5. Voucher System

True leadership must be strong from the top down.

The voucher system might shake up some of the thinking in the public schools. I truly believe our public schools would rise to the challenge of providing quality education if put to the test, but if not, a voucher system at least would give students the opportunity to attend a school that will serve their needs.

I realize my endorsement of vouchers is contrary to accepted public education doctrine, which holds that vouchers simply hasten the flight from public schools by the best and brightest; but I believe that a phase-in of vouchers would challenge *all* schools to

a) hire the best qualified teachers, paying top wages for knowledgeable, certified, highly rated teachers (rated by peers, principals, and students, if possible)

b) provide the best curriculum, with up-to-date textbooks and materials as tools for the creative teachers

c) inspire and encourage parents and students to carefully choose the environment most conducive to learning, given their unique needs

d) increase parental involvement in and assessment of the quality of their child's education, rather than (as now) abdicating responsibility for their child's future based on geographical neighborhood school proximity regardless of the actual quality of that individual school

e) assess funds to upgrade libraries with new books, tapes, and computers; bring in qualified guest speakers; and assure adequate school supplies (paints, crayons, paper, globes, etc) without making the teachers responsible for paying for them out of their own pockets.

6. Have a well-thought-out prevention program for students at risk, helping them <u>up</u> rather than discouraging them through punishment; make time to *listen* to teachers and students and staff; take time to show them respect and give them positive feedback.

7. Hold workshops on
   a) Humor as part of win/win situations; and
   b) Adjusting curriculum to fit students' needs (learning from mistakes)

8. Hold a monthly faculty pot-luck to share valuable success stories, to network with peers on problems and offer constructive suggestions.

9. Hold a workshop in which Administrators *listen* – with open minds, non-defensive attitudes and a sense of humor – to what teachers have to say about where the snags lie that prevent positive results.

My own experience suggests that, although administrators honestly believe they are open-minded and receptive to teachers' input and teachers' needs – psychological as well as material and curriculum-related – many administrators are anything but receptive to new ideas that would require delegation of control, or would involve positive rewards and encouragement for teachers.

Teachers feel trapped by rules and regulations, and by fears for the security of their jobs; they pass on this atmosphere of discontent to their students. A good administrator should never "put up" with this situation, and the whole concept of mutual respect and responsibility should reinforce the sense of administrators and teachers as members of the same team.

A retreat – away from school, and including a facilitator – would be an excellent way to give administrators and teachers a fresh venue to permit well-intentioned dialogue to open the gates to creative, meaningful solutions for today's troubled education system. A flexible, non-threatening atmosphere that encourages negotiation might be the path to making the right decisions for the right reasons.

Just as parents are guides and not owners of their children, so administrators should be guides for teachers – encouraging each teacher to do what he and she does best in the best way possible. Rather than expecting a blanket format to suit all teachers, let the expert practice his or her expertise. Teachers need to be encouraged and supported to take calculated risks, to keep their creative skills fresh, rather than being trapped in an administrator's preconceived expectations at the expense of innovative thinking.

In turn, teachers must regard administrators as team-members rather than "power hungry dictators" or adversaries. Every administrator would profit from being required to teach at least one class every year or two, to keep them in touch with the real world they aim to supervise.

It is time for administrators and teachers to set aside power politics, jealousies, greed, and control, and join forces to learn from one another, to make all parties winners in the magic of education. Let us formulate a plan, present it with room for feedback and individual adjustment, evaluate the results with the wisdom and courage to accept what works and re-think what doesn't, test and re-test to verify that we are offering the best possible curriculum, and keep our eyes on the goal of equipping our young people for a quality life.

This performance-based assessment must appeal to all parties involved – student, teacher, parent, administrator, school board, and community at large; this makes for an unbeatable team, and demonstrates that these efforts are worthy of funding.

The Personal Touch in Teaching: Reaching across the distance that separates us and uniting all those who truly understand the priceless gift that is education.

10. Tenure vs. Merit System

Having taught for more than thirty-five years, I am convinced that we should eliminate tenure and adopt the merit system. Too many teachers do not keep up with the times – they rest on their laurels of seniority. I have believed from the very first that good things sell themselves, and if they are not good enough, they should be eliminated.

This goes double for teaching – the most important resource of a nation. As for when and how to evaluate the teacher, may I suggest a panel made up of

a) the principal
b) an independent group of teachers who would evaluate the success of the subject offered
c) a group of counselors
d) a group of parents
e) a group of students

all of whom must be carefully chosen for their knowledge, integrity and fairness.

Teachers should be given every opportunity to be praised and rewarded for good teaching and helped and supported to correct weak points in their method. Only after an appropriate period of support to improve weak points should a teacher be given a warning, followed by an interval for improvement (suitably praised and rewarded based on merit) and only if improvement is inadequate, based on clearly outlined performance objectives, should a dismissal notice be given.

11. On Counselors

Counselors have to a great extent relinquished active *counseling* to become paper shufflers. They are asked to create charts to choose classes for students and similar busywork.

Let secretaries worry about charts, and let counselors *counsel.* More than any other single thing, today's students need someone to listen to them, and provide them with workable alternatives to solve their problems.

A monthly "Counselors' Round Table" could be a positive way to help identify and explore the students' needs.

I would also suggest enlisting a corps of strong, successful students as mentors for their classmates who need help; these mentors should be recognized by something such as a special plaque in a prominent location in the main corridor, for all to see and appreciate.

12. Courtship of Education

Since education is a cooperative effort among parents, teachers, counselors, administrators and students, I suggest the following forms of recognition for these "team players:"

Photos-of-the-Month of a parent, a teacher, a counselor, and a student, with a description of the contribution each individual has made to the school and the learning experience during the month; these photos could be posted in the main corridor, near the school office.

A special dinner, sponsored by the business community, for the administrator, principal, parent, teacher and counselor of the month (planned by the parent/teacher association).

13.   Concerning the Arts

The arts are the perfect means to nourish the soul, the spirit, the sensitivity, and the creativity in each individual. It is of utmost importance to offer as many opportunities as possible to all students to enjoy the arts, to avoid turning out a multitude of robots.

I would suggest inviting artists, art schools, museums and benefactors to sponsor

- a) a basic system-wide school arts program
- b) a wide range of opportunities to attend arts performances and events
- c) art scholarships for those exhibiting talent
- d) work-study positions and professional placement assistance for arts graduates

14.   About Science

Science offers critical thinking, discipline, order, and creativity to students. I would suggest

- a) a Science Round Table, where teachers, students, and scientists in the community can meet and exchange ideas
- b) a Science Contribution plaque, recognizing the science students' special contributions
- c) counselors could let recognized local and regional scientists know about the up-and-coming young scientists in our schools, and/or arrange for an on-

the-job meeting between the scientist and his laboratory and the gifted science students.

15. On Business

Match businesses with promising business students. Arrange for businesses to invite these students to lunch and for tours of their business sites, to share ideas and possibly offer business assistantships and other opportunities to these students. Recognize those students' contributions with a photo and a description of their activities in a prominent place at the school.

16. Community Involvement

In an annual assembly, invite the mayor and the city commissioners to the school; pair these officials with the recognized Student-of-the-Month, Teacher-of-the-Month, etc.

Ask the city to present specific job experiences to the students (a park superintendent, water bureau director, traffic planning engineer, river patrol officer, and/or chief of police could be invited to speak to a student assembly about the actual working of his or her department), or arrange student tours of city offices.

Students could be encouraged to keep a journal of these experiences, with comments to share with fellow students; these journals could then be shared with the city.

* * *

Madame with her students at Klamath Union High School,
Klamath Falls, Oregon

Last day of school at Benson High School

Madame. Amélie Diamant-Holmstrom with her colleagues Dr. Fredrick
G. Rodgers, Mr. Hill Hughes and Mr. Robin Hill from Benson High
School in Portland, Oregon "I am retiring from full time teaching but
I'll be back substituting. For me teaching is a passion"

"Retirement is but the beginning of a new venture.
When one door closes, another door opens."

In the interest of our students it is essential that teachers court parents
and that parents court teachers. It takes good will and an open mind
and heart to do so.

Message for teachers

Dear Teachers:

Permit me to suggest you offer these **life skills** from my *Courtship of Life* to your students. They are the guideposts of a quality life:

1. GIVE generously, freely, from the heart, with no strings attached
2. RECEIVE with joy and gratitude
3. OBSERVE, IDENTIFY, ASSESS, REFINE, and EVALUATE your place in the world
4. LISTEN, SEE, TOUCH and use each of your senses to absorb and appreciate Life
5. COMMUNICATE your thoughts, ideas, feelings in a positive, sensitive, clear way
6. ENJOY each day as a new opportunity to succeed
7. SHARE your joy in life with others

To be effective teachers

1. Make your classroom a pleasant, meaningful, inviting place where thoughtful human beings teach and learn and work together.
2. Greet the students, by name, at the door, saying something positive.
3. Treat your students with respect, as important individuals, and insist they treat themselves and each other in the same manner.

4. Offer a suitable curriculum, pertinent and involving to the students' intellect, appropriate to their needs, and worthy of their time and yours.

5. Cultivate your students' thirst for knowledge, and reward their initiative and effort.

6. Maintain the highest standards of integrity, responsibility, and courage.

7. Teach patience, tolerance, cooperation and positive problem solving.

8. Enjoy the rewards of your hard work!

Notes

_____

_____

_____

_____

_____

_____

_____

_____

_____

_____

_____

_____

_____

_____

_____

_____

_____

_____

_____

Madame at her home with her students planning a fundraiser
"There is always a way to help, to improve, to further and
to enrich education."

Fund raising ideas you can use for your school

1. Promote a monthly fun and meaningful WALK FOR EDUCATION (around the school, or around the track field, etc.)
   a) students could sponsor teachers
   b) teachers could sponsor students
   c) parents could sponsor students and/or teachers
   d) end the experience with a group-sing of a special song – such as my "Love Lights The City" – this will keep the Walk for Education connected to the group and (hopefully) help it become a tradition.

2. Offer summer-camp scholarships for needy students; funds could be raised by compiling an International COOKBOOK (each student could contribute a favorite recipe of their family, and the Business department could assemble it)

3. Each student could be asked to bring a QUILT SQUARE (depicting a drawing, collage, poem, proverb, etc) for the parent teacher association to stitch together and raffle off as a Collector's Quilt.

4. Administrators, teachers and parents could organize a SILENT AUCTION of donated items – art work, crafts, food items, flower arrangements, books, services, weekend getaways, etc – in connection with

an interesting film (video), or a skit or play by students, etc.

Let's think of ways to have fun while raising needed funds for our schools! We are all each other's keepers – let's all help each other look better than we are!

Notes

To live a quality life one must take time to smell the flowers.

My final thoughts and philosophy and teaching

To the Administrator, Teacher, Counselor, Parent, Mentor and Caregiver:

Be a leader
Be a guide
Be a path-finder
Be a co-pilot
Be a friend, not a buddy
Be a thinker
Be a doer
Be energetically communicative
Be reflective
Be responsible
Be informed
Be well organized
Be confident
Be observant
Be trustworthy
Be reliable
Be tolerant
Be flexible
Be consistent
Be able to take calculated risks
Be able to teach your students how to take calculated risks
Be able to clarify situations and problems
Be able to help your students to clarify situations and problems

Have command of the subject
Have a positive attitude
Have love and respect for the individual and for knowledge
Have a clear understanding of each student's ability and limits
Have the skill to meet the student's needs

I wish you success in your journey,

Please Respond With Your Comments:

Teachers, parents, students, counselors, administrators:
Please feel free to comment with constructive feedback, and add whatever you have to contribute to keep improving our educational system for the sake of our students. The only constant in life is change, if we want to keep excellence alive and growth continuous.

Send your input or requests to:

Amélie Diamant-Holmstrom
P.O. Box 18208
Portland, OR 97218

PORTLAND PUBLIC SCHOOLS
546 Northeast 12th Avenue / Portland, Oregon 97232
Phone. (503) 280-5100.

BENSON HIGH SCHOOL

Office of the Principal

March 4, 1987

To Whom It May Concern:

I have been asked to write a letter of recommendation for Amelie Holmstrom. Frankly, I am tempted to write something vaguely sinister so no one else will hire her away from Benson.

Mme. Holmstrom is a vibrant and eclectic personality. She is a "character" in the finest sense of the term. She presents a world view of compassion, integration, and common sense. She makes a lasting impression on students as she strives to have each student recognize and work toward their potential.

She is not a strict disciplinarian and most of the time, she doesn't need to be. Her strengths lie in convincing students that it is in their best interest to participate in class and she does this very well.

She communicates very well with parents since she takes such a sincere interest in their children.

Her approach to teaching language is through culture. She incorporates food, song, dance and cultural ritual in her classes. She willingly spends time outside of class involving students in language related experiences.

She is a willing faculty volunteer for activities such as curriculum development and United Way.

Mme. Holmstrom does not fit most of the commonly held stereotypes about school teachers. She is not reserved or prim, she is vital and exhuberant. She is not always prudent, she is always enthusiastic; she is not rigid and conforming, she is flexible and seeks flexibility. She is an interesting and interested person.

I realize this is an unusual letter of recommendation, but it fits Amelie.

Sincerely,

Carol Matarazzo

thank you for
helping me
over grow
the government.

Thank-you for being so
understanding and compassionate
Dottie

You are a great inspiration,
an obvious loving woman,
filled with a mixture
of compassion, zest for
life, and love. Thank
you,
Simone Cimiluca

GRANT HIGH SCHOOL
PORTLAND, OREGON
5/14/2002

your kindness and love
for the world inspires
every student you come
to teach. Thank you
Kira Donnelly

GRANT HIGH SCHOOL
PORTLAND, OREGON 5/14/02

much love

your viewpoints on life
were so encouraging to me
in just the short time
you were here. Hope to
see you again.
David Vail

I'm glad you were
our substitute.
Tran Stromy

Anthony Frison

your the kindness substitute
in the world. You bring
happiness to each and every
one of u.

Thank you so much
for sharing your love
with the rest of
the world. It is encouraging
to know that there are
people like you, out in
the world. Thank you,
Joanna Ames

Athanasio
Kondilis

It is great having
you as a teacher
you show each kid
love and always lent
a helping hand when
it is needed. It is
a great book
Paul Slawk

You are an
awesome role
model for men,
women, and
children of all
ages. Thank
you!

Menu Holet amme personno
Madame sus magnifica
luis eres magnifica essa landecia

Having you as a
teacher makes each
class a little more
enriching and enjoyable
thank you for giving me the
opportunity to experience
your wisdom
Matt Wallace

Thanks for
showing so much
love for us others
around us. I hope your
inspirational attitude will
be around our community
for many more years.
Drew Smithers

You're so amazing. Your
story of your children inspired
me to become a better
person. I'm pleased to
have had you as a mentor.
—André Nakazawa—

An inspirational writer
inspires generations to
come. Effect may now
love's and beyond the future.
with love
Ashwood

You speak inspirational
and encouraging words that
opens all ears to hear
what you say. thank
you so much for coming
to our school. I hope
to see you again.
Kristine Franz

thank you so much for being
such an inspiring soul. Good-
luck with sharing your
message and love; you are a
blessing. Celeste Arias

had you as a substitute and I have enjoyed you so much! You infect everyone with joy and an inspiration to teach.
Grace O. Uwagbae

Your enthusiasm for teaching and for life in general instills in us our own motivation to tackle the next moments in life. Thank you so much.
Noel Miller

Thank You, Eshet

I have enjoyed your teaching.
Thank you very much for your inspiration.
Your passion for teaching is great
— Sam D.

as a farmer you work hard for the benefit of all, as a samurai you risk yourself for the well being of few.
— Sri Benson

I have enjoyed your teaching very much. The love behind your words is inspiring.
Thank you for a life of learning

Your compassion for love and life is boundless. I learn something new about life everytime you teach my class. Your an inspiration and an amazing woman. It would be a full time experience if I had you as a life time teacher.
— Nathan Pawley

You are passionate about life, and embody possibilities. Thanks for helping uncover our infinitude of possibilities.
Lola Milkweed

GRANT HIGH SCHOOL

PORTLAND OREGON 5/14/02

I enjoy your stories
thank You!
Chris Kewie

You are the best Sub I have ever had. You have taught me more about life in one class than I could ever imagine. Thank you so much. I hope that your knowledge + inspiration flows throughout this community for many more years.
— Jess Hims

Like anyone really understood how anyone would want to be a substitute teacher, but the time being in your class you proved me how I was better. On substituting and now I was relieved to see someone aspire to get as fulfilling it is for you, as I aspire to get as much zeal and passion you had been do in yours. Knowing you has given me a greater appreciation that will stay with me forever.
Thank you.
Neysa Shidyer

It's nice to know that someone aches in my generation.
Thank you.
And remember: Our imaginations fires. We are out its shadows on the earth.
Rayn McMahon

You are the only substitute I have ever had that immediately puts a smile on my face. Keep spreading joy to students everywhere!
~EMILY KROPP

You take the time and enjoy giving encouragement to students. That's good because sometimes we really need it.
Christine Coleman

About the Author

Amélie Diamant Holmstrom is inspiring, empowering and thought provoking. As a teacher, author, seminar leader and personal consultant she is a visionary and a force of nature."

Professor Robert Politzer (ret.)

Stanford University.

Amélie Diamant Holmstrom has been a teacher for more than thirty years. She has taught French at the University of Washington in Seattle and in Oregon. She was formerly chair of Foreign Languages at Roosevelt Junior High School and Del Valle High School in California, and at Klamath Falls, Benson and Grant High Schools in Oregon.

She is co-author, with noted linguist, Professor Robert Politzer, of *French: A Creative Approach* (American Book Company, 1970).

Two other books currently available in *The Courtship of Life* series: *Conversations with Thomas* designed to foster meaningful and enjoyable communication between parents, grandparents, caretakers, mentors and children, and *Yes, I Can!* which guides, motivates and inspires the individual to live life to it's full potential with joy, meaning and satisfaction. It is a blueprint to leading a QUALITY LIFE!

For further information,
contact Amélie Diamant Holmstrom at
Box 18208,
Portland, Oregon 97218.

*Destined for
Greatness*

A new kind of young adult
book for students,
teachers, administrators,
counselors, and parents.

Author Amélie Diamant Holmstrom discusses her ideas on living, teaching, and parenting at one of her many lecture appearances.

CPSIA information can be obtained
at www.ICGtesting.com
Printed in the USA
FFHW020514081119
56014570-61893FF